What We All Want to Say

Poetry for grades 6-12

Elizabeth Crocket

For all young people who find their voice through poetry.

And my six grandchildren, who fill me with gratitude.

Foreword

The time we spend in school up to and including High School is a time that is rich with new experiences. Friendships with students and teachers, sports, and the continuing importance of language both spoken and written are critical to us when we grow into what is called adulthood. In point of fact what is called youth stays with us for the rest of our lives. There is angst, there is lost love, there are authority figures who annoy and sometimes mistreat or misjudge you throughout your life. Haiku and senryu are truly a journal of your life.

In this collection, Elizabeth Crocket has given us a glimpse into her past, and into her future. For better or for worse we carry with us all of the experiences in our life. They are though much less of a burden if they are in the form of a poem. Haiku are short poems that are small reminders of the larger issues in life. Look at them as bookmarks for the larger event stored in your memory.

Michael Rehling

on my back
the weight of
all they want me to be

first kiss
a butterfly chooses
the flower

sick day
an overcrowded
mind

open door
the security
of grandma's house

break-up
a bird rips through
the spider web

ATV race
mud
on my face

another teacher
picking
on me

designer clothes
the expense
of cool

high price
a nod
from the wrong group

low grades
pretending
to care

report card
mom and dad tag-team
new ideas

sports night
pushing me
through today

ringing bell
the best sound
of the day

California poppy
a lone fist rises
then another and another

parent-teacher interview
siblings measure
how they did

sick day
friends cover
my tracks

cute guy
only visits
in my dreams

mom's smile
wondering
who she used to be

photo album
so many pictures
of my older brother

rough day
in the dog's eyes
understanding

lesson learned
no bedtime
when reading

lunch hour
finding warmth
from my thermos

at school
my worries
at home

leaving for school
staying with me
dad's pat on the back

poetry class
creating a good thing
from a bad thing

backpack
the teacher pulls out
disappointment

new kid
the buzz
of every phone

first A
trying hard
not to grin

parent-teacher night
the discussion
follows us home

out of control party
the unexpected guest
my dad

Good Read

I never told the kids in my class that I loved to read and write. How I'd just devour a book instead of dinner. After school, I stand before the teacher and ask if she would mind reading a story I'd written. You know, for feedback.

poker face
a teacher still
reads me

animals
the teacher leaves
the classroom

tissues on our noses
the principle's
b.o.

funny kid
he gets to tell his joke
in the office

Looking Up

I gaze out the window, as the walls of the classroom are closing in. I wonder what we're doing cooped up in here when we could be outside on this warm spring day. I can't believe my ears when I hear the teacher say that gym class will be held outside today. A loud chorus of, "Yessss" fills the room.

a baseball
the slow glide
towards the sun

Different Goals

The teacher screeches like a barn owl. "Whatever you are daydreaming about couldn't possibly be as important as this." She points at the blackboard crowded with information that has no relevance to my life. A smirk pulls at my lip, like a lopsided window blind, as her voice becomes higher.

ice on the pond
the sound
of new skates

after school
all the activities
I never chose

end of day
the emptiness
in the detention room

low battery
so many friends
lonely

kids left in charge
making out
in the cloakroom

school dance
the prettiest girl
sits alone

Christmas holidays
my uncle includes me
in his rant

cold rain
for the first time
I see dad cry

summer holidays
my family
rides the waves

party invitation
praying my parents
won't let me go

last report card
sliding into
a new home base

not chosen for choir
still
we sing

after music class
she choreographs
her squeegee

low flying kites
teenagers
in a pandemic

first paycheque
walking taller
in these shoes

listening for my date
the old motorcycle
baffles

autistic student
screaming out
what we all want to say

9 789390 202386